MOMENTS WITH THE MASTER

MOMENTS WITH THE MASTER

A Reflective Time

Linda J. Humes

To order additional copies of this book, contact:
Xlibris Corporation
1-888-7-XLIBRIS
www.Xlibris.com
Orders@Xlibris.com

CONTENTS

This book is dedicated to my husband, Tom, my children Paul, Elisha and Jonathan, and to my family in faith at the River of Life Church.

Without their encouragement and support, this book would be nothing more than bits of paper in a desk drawer.

PROLOGUE

There are times when we seek God for wisdom for a situation. There are times when we cry out to God in intercession for a loved one. There are times when we humbly kneel before God for peace over our circumstances. Then there are times when we quietly sit, talk, praise and meditate on His Holy Word. Times when we intimately share with God our true appreciation for His precious daily gifts.

It is during these precious, intimate *"Moments With The Master"* that He tenders our hearts to hear His loving voice. During those moments we are touched with inspiration and revelation of His greatness.

This book is dedicated to those moments and the wisdom He has shared. Find a quiet place, begin with prayer and enjoy the tender words of hope inspired by The Master.

TENDER BUDS

Let not your heart be troubled: ye believe in God, believe also in
me. [2] In my Father's house are many mansions: if it were not
so, I would have told you. I go to prepare a place for you.
John 14:1-2 KJV

How splendid, Lord, the flow of Your words,
Delightful, they float through my days.
How precious the promise I carry within,
As I walk and I live in Your ways.

How tender the souls that search for the joy,
That only Your children can know.
How blessed the moments of sharing God's love,
And watching those tender buds grow.

MY PRECIOUS FATHER

To appoint unto them that mourn in Zion, to give unto them beauty for ashes, the oil of joy for mourning, the garment of praise for the spirit of heaviness; that they might be called trees of righteousness, the planting of the Lord, that he might be glorified.

Isaiah 61:3 KJV

I have a precious Father,
Who is always there for me.
Not one minute of the day goes by,
When I can't see Him and all He's done.
A Father whose lap I can nestle in,
When I'm feeling tired or overwhelmed;
Where I can grieve and mourn,
And feel peace as His strong arms,
Shroud me with His Glory.

I have a precious Father,
Who never leaves my side.
He provides the joy in my happiness,
He provides the strength in my sadness.
He gives me the freedom of decisions,
And the mercy of forgiveness,
When my decisions are poor.

I have a precious Father,
Who provides the sunlight of my mornings,
A cool breeze in the heat of the day,

And the brightness of silvery stars in a blackened night.
My Father paints the sky,
With the rise and set of the sun,
And dances the clouds about,
For my pleasure.

I have a precious Father,
Who holds the wealth of Kings,
In the palm of His hand.
Who lifts the broken out of poverty,
Lays waste the Kingdoms of the self-righteous.

And in all His greatness and majesty,
My precious Father,
Never forgets me,
Never sets me aside,
Never leaves me for a moment,
Even in times when I am less than thoughtful.
A precious Father that will remain with me,
All the days of my life,
Even though I choose,
To walk away from Him.

I have a precious Father,
Who will grant me the wisdom,
And bless me with the anointing,
To remain in His will,
Protecting His legacy,
In my meager way,
Always remembering,
That I have a precious Father.

A NEW DAY

We have also a more sure word of prophecy; whereunto ye do well
that ye take heed, as unto a light that shineth in a dark place,
until the day dawn, and the day star arise in your hearts:
2 Peter 1:19 KJV

You take the darkness of night,
Through the chill of dawn,
And burst forth the morning sky,
Opening in fragrant gold,
As a beautiful yellow rose bud,
Firm yet delicate,
Opening its vulnerable petals,
To bless the waiting soul.

The colors race across the sky,
Painted by the wings of Angels.
The sun rises,
Orchestrating warmth and life,
Bringing hope.

It's a new day!

And as these miracles of morning,
These miracles of life,
Explode all around,
So many pass right by,
Unaware.

My Spirit cries out,
"Look what God has done,
Look what He has made for you."
They pass right by,
Unaware.

Let me always cling,
To the miracles of the moment,
Always aware,
Always grateful,
For the hand of God.

THIS HOUSE

And if it seem evil unto you to serve the Lord, choose you this day whom ye will serve; whether the gods which your fathers served that were on the other side of the flood, or the gods of the Amorites, in whose land ye dwell: but as for me and my house, we will serve the Lord.

Joshua 24:15 KJV

This house which stands is humble.
The outside is simple—neat.
It does not command attention,
It does not exalt wealth.

Yet, this house has become a home,
Each inch dedicated to the Gospel.
Look inside with the eyes of a Saint,
Past the aging tapestries,
Past the dull, sparse paint.

This house glows in Gold,
From the essence of His Glory within.
It is laden with silver,
From the Light of the Son.
Every inch is warmed,
By the love of His children.
It is shielded and draped,
In the Armor of Righteousness.

This house which stands is humble.
The outside is simple—neat.

But this home which we've built is great,
For it houses the Mighty Living God.
This God which cannot be contained,
Not by strength,
Not by boundaries,
Not by false sacrifice.
But which chooses to dwell,
In a sanctuary of praise,
Raised by the hearts of His own.

INTIMACY

*And God saw every thing that he had made, and, behold, it
was very good. And the evening and the morning were the sixth
day.*

Genesis 1:31 KJV

The sweet breath of spring
    rises up to greet the
    pure, first light of dawn.

The fields dance,
    stirring silent butterflies,
    rising to decorate the sky.

The seas surge and recede,
    calling to the waking earth,
    It's a new day!

Resting there,
receive the gift,
of the innocence born of God,
of the intimacy known with God.

JUDAH

Judah, thou art he whom thy brethren shall praise: thy hand shall be in the neck of thine enemies; thy father's children shall bow down before thee.

Genesis 49:8 KJV

Judah is rising up,
    As the Phoenix Bird from her ashes,
    Reborn and Refreshed,
    To take His place in the line of war.

His dead are walking forth from the tombs,
    where they have been wrapped,
    In the works of this world.

The scales are being removed from
    His blinded eyes,
    Falling to His feet of bronze.

His tongue is being loosed,
    To bring the message of God.

*Judah is rising up to take His place
in the line of war.*

With the blessing of Jacob,
    And the prayer of Moses,
    He prepares Himself,

Ready to battle,
In the Armor of Light.

The belt of truth glistens in the light of the sun,
Making a way,
Distilling the darkness.

Righteousness adorns His breast,
Truth, Grace, Justice.

Peace from the written Word,
Which <u>was</u> God and <u>is</u> God,
Steadies and guides His feet.

Cloaked with faith,
Which no evil can penetrate.

Covering His head with the Anointing oil,
A Spiritual helmet,
Cleansing the mind,
Clearing the confusion,
Making salvation clear.

Stepping forth in the strength of the Spirit,
Both violent and tender,
Judging in Love,
He begins the walk.

Judah has risen,
He is taking His place,
In this Spiritual War.

The singers march first,
To anoint the field,
Causing demons to flee.

The Levites remain, interceding,
　　Protecting, lighting the way,
　　With prayers unceasing.

Those that have fallen,
　　Those that have strayed,
　　Hear His call.

The Lion roars in the tribe of Judah,
　　The Root of David gains strength.

The songs of Angels' tongues break forth,
　　Screams and gnashing echo
　　in the darkness.

Judah has risen, He has taken His place.

TAKE MY HAND

"Thou leddest thy people like a flock by the hand of Moses and Aaron."

Psalm 77:20 KJV

Take my hand, Lord,
    and guide me through this weary time.

Gently lift and gently lead,
    my eyes are tired,
    the path is dim.

Take my hand, Lord,
    a grasp of friendship,
    a grasp of love.

Father to child,
    child to father,
    trusting,
    secure,
    warm.

Take my hand, Lord,
    that I might be healed,
    and capable soon,
    to reach my hand,
    back to another.

LETTING GO

Cast thy burden upon the Lord, and he shall sustain thee: he shall never suffer the righteous to be moved.

Psalm 55:22 KJV

I have a big Bible, Giant Print. The kind that is so easy to read that you spend all of your study time in it, but so big and bulky that you never it carry it to Church Services or study classes. It's the big lunky study Bible, with pages falling out, and bled through highlighting (often making it difficult to figure out which side of the page held the vast important Rhema message of the moment). The Bible with the pictures of loved ones, their needs written on the back. The Bible with the prayer lists from years back and notes from a special sermon, dog-eared and marked from hours of digging. It's the one with the family tree, the births and deaths, the baptism dates, salvation dates, and the day my son uttered in tongues for the first time.

The Bible I use as a pillow when I pray myself to sleep while walking through the valley. The one with coffee stains made one excited morning when God met our need, when we once more stood high upon the mountain. The one with every promise underlined and Psalm 23 in the upper left hand column of the right page.

You know which one I mean. We all have one. Mine has become so very special to me. It is the first thing packed in my suitcase and the first thing removed when I arrive at my destination. It's the first thing I read in the morning and the last thing I read at night, no matter where I travel.

Recently I took it to a Woman's Retreat. Although it shared my study time in the chapel library and made a few trips to the pond, it didn't go to the services. It was much too important. It holds, tucked carefully inside, my precious treasures.

As I was folding it up one morning, it slipped from my grip and dozens of papers fell out. I carefully, gently, picked each one up and relived the emotions of the prayer requests or notes written thereon. It was a wonderful lift in my faith as I realized that all but a few of those requests had already been fulfilled. Years of requests ranging from what now seems so small, to what will always be overwhelming. All needs and desires met by God's mercy and grace.

When I had a request which seemed so large to my immediate circumstance, I wrote it down. I told God that it was too big for me and I was tucking it in amongst His promises. It was a time of humbling myself, admitting that I could not meet my own needs. It was a time of letting go.

As I read through those notes I saw where I had made notes and dates about when those needs were met. Needs for groceries, met within a day. Needs for a car, met within a month, free and clear. Needs for a house, met within six months, free and clear. Even the desire for fresh fruit when we had eaten food bank canned fruit for so long, met within an hour. God knew just what to do. He answered our needs exceedingly, abundantly above all I could have expected.

Is it a magic Bible? A special prayer formula? Special anointed paper? An anointed pen? NO! It was stepping back and letting God fulfill the promises He so graciously gave us. It was getting out of His way. Our Blessed God who met all our needs, and a few simple desires—like the taste and texture of a fresh peach. It was simply letting go.

A PERFECT HEART

*And he said unto him, Son, thou art ever with me, and all that
I have is thine. [32] It was meet that we should make merry,
and be glad: for this thy brother was dead, and is alive again;
and was lost, and is found.*

Luke 15:31-32 KJV

Where is my heart, Lord,
The heart You can see.
Has it wandered much too far,
From where it ought to be?

I rest in Your presence
And wonder where I am.
Have I gone too far?
Have I given up too soon?
You have set a path for me,
Charted by Grace,
Out of bondage,
Through the Wilderness,
Into the Promised Land.

How often do I cast a glance
At the familiar security of bondage?
My memories, sweetened with time,
Draw me back across the Wilderness
That I have already overcome.
My promise of tomorrow,

Looses distance,
By my own temptations.

Yet, at the end of my daily journey,
As I cry out,
You rest with me.
Words of encouragement urge me forward,
The reality of temptation, once again,
Becomes clear.

There is no anger in your voice,
There is no disappointment,
Only tears of joy,
Fatherly pride,
As I step, once again,
Toward the promise.

Callous my heart, Lord,
To sweetened memories,
To familiarity.

Tender my hear, Lord, toward You.
Let me see Your path with certainty.
Harness my mind and confusion.
Touch the greatest depths of my soul,
That when we meet again,
In the cool of the day,
That I might hear You,
With a perfect heart.

BIRTH OF THE BRIDE

And Adam said, This is now bone of my bones, and flesh of my flesh: she shall be called Woman, because she was taken out of Man.

Genesis 2:23 KJV

The waters came forth,
    pure and abundant,
    preparing for life,
    supernaturally.

The evening and the morning,
    were the 5th day,
    life had begun.

From the dust of the dry land,
    and the waters of the sea,
    God's hand formed and molded man,
    the first Adam.

The blood in his body lay silent,
    His image and soul lay pure,
    without life, water and blood ran together,
    unheedingly.

Then into his nostrils did God breathe,
    true life,
    not merging liquid,
    not hardened soil.

The gentle breeze from the soul of God,
    drew man to life,
    away from silent existence,
    covenant of love,
    covenant of truth.

The blood and water coursed within man,
    birthing forth the desire,
    of a new covenant.

In the safety of love man rested,
    a deep sleep,
    peaceful sleep.

God reached deep inside,
    removing a small sacrifice,
    blood and water and molded dust.

This rib became the bride of Adam,
    still and lifeless,
    breathed to life,
    by the same precious deity,
    the one Holy God.

By the breath of God did the woman rise,
    from mere existence,
    to precious life.

She was to bear the cycle,
    the covenant of blood and water,
    the temporary temple of God's chosen.

The cycle continued,
    covenant—sacrifice,
    birth—sacrifice,
    covenant—death.

Jesus, the final covenant,
    God the son,
    the covenant of eternal life,
    the Bride of Christ.

Even in death,
    precious blood and water,
    amniotic fluid ran down the cross,
    onto a cursed hill—Golgatha.

With it ran the seed of a new nation,
    a new generation,
    the covenant of eternal life,
    the Bride of Christ.

With His last earthly breath,
    He drew in the sins of the world,
    and the Bride to come,
    that all life might dwell,
    in the Holy promises.

The sins, cleansed and forgiven,
    ran with the blood,
    ran with the water,
    planting the seed,
    of the covenant to come,
    Kingdom Heirs.

A tiny baby, born in the darkest of times,
    nurtured by the hand of God,
    filled with the breath of the Spirit,
    coursed through with sacrificial blood,
    sacrificial water.

No longer apart from God the Father,
    no longer apart from God the Son,
    the miraculous testimony of living Word,
    birthed in the death of sin.

Rise up, Oh Israel,
    take your inheritance of life,
    God breathed,
    Holy & Blessed.

Clothe yourself in gold and purple,
    as the rightful Bride,
    of Christ.

Rise up, Oh Israel,
    for the Groom prepares the place,
    where you shall dwell,
    the promises have come to pass,
    where faith met truth,
    and they become one.

WHAT DO YOU SEE

*For thou hast possessed my reins: thou hast covered me in my
mother's womb.*

Psalm 139:13 KJV

Lord,
In the drifting tides of time—you knew me.
You were preparing a way—for such a time as this.
What do you see in this tarnished,
    broken vessel.
Why did you give so very,
    very much for me.
What do you see, Lord?
What do you see?

My Child,
I see the saints—generations passed—paving a way for
you.
I see your family—speaking God's Word -
    protecting your days.
I see a child growing—strong in me -
    strong In love—strong in compassion.
I see a vessel of clay—not broken, but repaired.
I see a tender heart—humbled by a life of trials—
    fought and conquered—through me.

And I see tarnished, broken vessels -
　　waiting for you -
　　to breathe hope and life—
　　into them.

I see you, Child—going forth -
　　to be my hands, my words -
　　repairing those tarnished broken vessels.

Just as another came to you -
　　the night you first called -
　　My Name.

FEAR NOT

*And the angel said unto her, Fear not, Mary: for thou hast
found favour with God.*

Luke 1:30 KJV

In the bosom of innocence lay a mighty seed,
    Kissed by Deity,
    Torn from the safety of Heaven,
    Planted by the hand of God.

Fear not, Mary, for within you rises a mighty nation,
    Within you rests the end of death,
    The keys to life.

Ten tiny fingers, ten little toes,
    A mind that reads the multitudes,
    A soul absent of sin.

Innocence bearing innocence,
    Purity rising forth,
    In humble servitude.

Fear not, Mary,
    For the walk of faith,
    The sacrifices to come,
    Will be met with Grace,
    Sent from the Father above.

Fear not for the pain so deep,
    That only a mother could know,
    That only a mother could bear.

Fear not for that one small child,
    Held up by the arms of the father,
    Given back to God.

Fear not, Mary, for the blood to be shed,
    For the wooden tree,
    That holds Him up to God,
    In a mocking, cynical taunt.

Fear not, Mary,
    For the tears and confusions of the day,
    Make way for the joy of the risen savior,
    Untouched by death,
    Sitting at the right hand of the Father.

Rejoice, Mary, for the precious times,
    You held Him close,
    For the pride you felt,
    As He touched the crowds.

Rejoice, Mary,
    That for all His attempts,
    Satan was bruised,
    And banished,
    To rule the dead.

Rejoice, Mary,
    For the precious Grace,
    That met your need,
    And the needs of the generations,
    Because of the innocence sacrificed,
    To the hand of God.

FOOTSTEPS

But Jesus called them unto him, and said, Suffer little children to come unto me, and forbid them not: for of such is the kingdom of God.

Luke 18:16 KJV

What manner of Saint must I be,
To follow in the footsteps of Christ.
What sort of war must I wage,
What must I give for the price.

Must I walk in the path of wealth,
Giving my treasure to find my way.
Must I earn every possible dime,
Letting riches pave my way.

Must I walk in the wisdom I've gained,
Sharing my thoughts and beliefs with all men.
To continue to search, to continue to learn,
To follow the path of the pen.

Or is it the path of helps,
Feed the poor and encourage the lost.
Will this bring the angels, to show me the way,
Will I walk with the Heavenly hosts.

Is it in learning Your Word and Your ways,
That Your steps will be revealed.

By quoting a verse, or by singing a Psalm,
Is this the way that's real?

Tell me Lord. What manner of Saint must I be?

"These are all good,"
Spoke the Lord's tender voice,
"And will help you to understand Me."
"But, the truth is so simple, so easy to follow,
"It's something that all Saints can be."

"Just step in My footsteps,
With the foot of a child,
Trusting, open and free."
"Step where they lead you,
Without weighing the odds,
At the last step you'll truly find Me."

RESTING WITH MARY

But one thing is needful: and Mary hath chosen that good part,
which shall not be taken away from her.

Luke 10:42 KJV

Forever in my mind rests the sweet fragrance
  of a summer rose,
The cool soft pedals caress the tips of my fingers,
The perfectly formed flower nestles gently in my memory
Ready to rise at a moments request.

Though the rose is gone,
The memory,
Ever much as sweet,
Cannot be taken away.

Then stands the Rose of Sharon
A tender fragrance rising sweetly in my soul.
A cool, soft caress that soothes my weary mind ,
And removes the torments of the day,
Nestled gently and preciously inside this child,
Where He cannot be taken away.

The words of the Master hide safely in my heart,
Prepared to flow forth in the time of need.
Lying safely in the arms of the Spirit,
Residing tenderly within this child.

Though the wooden structure of the Church,
May be destroyed,
And every book burned,
Inside this child rests a temple,
With God's Word, that cannot be taken away.

And though this body may be taken,
What victory, what joy -
For that which rests inside my heart and soul,
Will be brought to life in that Holy City,
When I meet Jesus, face to face.

FORGIVENESS

For if ye forgive men their trespasses, your heavenly Father will
also forgive you:

Matthew 6:14 KJV

There's a fire deep inside,
    That spreads,
    That dwindles,
    That spreads.

No one else can see it,
    No one else can feel it,
    But it eats like a canker,
    Into my peace.

Someone set the fuel in place,
    Another provided the spark,
    But I set the flame,
    I keep it alive.

It isn't a warming thing,
    Based on love,
    Although it replaced love,
    A long time ago.

It is a burning thing,
    Based on hate,
    I can't let go of,
    I won't let go.

And though I know,
>> Others can sense it,
>> Others shy from it,
>> I am the only one,
>> Who truly suffers.

As much as I want,
>> To be free of this sin,
>> It beacons me back,
>> It calls me friend.

It keeps me from growth,
>> It harnesses my joy,
>> It alters my path,
>> It chains me to me.

Lord, help me forgive,
>> The pains of the past,
>> That I might have freedom,
>> To live.

HUMBLE DILIGENCE

For verily I say unto you, Till heaven and earth pass, one jot or
one tittle shall in no wise pass from the law, till all be fulfilled.

Matthew 5:18 KJV

Against hardened hearts,
practiced tradition,
perverse generations,
- You stand.

Humble, yet determined,
Diligent, yet patient,
Tender, yet firm,
- You stand.

Weeping for souls lost in unbelief,
Weeping for generations to come,
Following the curse of their father,
Weeping for each and every battle
        that You are not prayed into.
Weeping for the souls that will not cry out,
- You stand.

Your Word does not change,
Your love, everlasting,
Your message is open and free,
You are life,
You are joy,
You are peace,

- You stand.

Diligently waiting,
- You stand.
Tenderly calling,
- You stand.
Lovingly listening,
- You stand.

Standing on truth,
Standing on the Word,
Standing on the side,
Waiting, For Me.

YOU'RE THERE

And he said, Go forth, and stand upon the mount before the Lord. And, behold, the Lord passed by, and a great and strong wind rent the mountains, and brake in pieces the rocks before the Lord; but the Lord was not in the wind: and after the wind an earthquake; but the Lord was not in the earthquake: [12] And after the earthquake a fire; but the Lord was not in the fire: and after the fire a still small voice.

1 Kings 19:11-12 KJV

I can't hear You, Lord,
I can't hear You today.
Just a quiet whispering;
A rustling.

There was a day when we walked together,
Talked together,
Closest friends.
Your words were loud and sure,
I knew Your will,
No doubt which path to take.
But I can't hear You, Lord,
I can't hear You today.

There were joyful times,
Times of tears,
Times of intercession,
And deepest prayers.
I felt You then,

You heard my cries and held me tight.
But I can't hear You, Lord,
I can't hear You today.

Somewhere I fell faint,
Neglected to listen,
Perhaps I disobeyed.
Or is this a testing time,
To see if I will remain,
Even in Your silence.
How will I know, Lord,
I can't hear You today.

I'll go on, as You've taught me,
I'll overcome,
Walk in joy,
Sing Your praises,
Again and again.
And when You've finished,
Testing and trying,
Pruning and purging,
Loving and lifting,
I will know.

Even in silence You are there,
Even in darkness You are there,
Even in diligent unanswered prayer,
You are there.
In Your word,
And in the hearts of Your children.

DEVIL'S TONGUES

For we wrestle not against flesh and blood, but against princi-
palities, against powers, against the rulers of the darkness of this
world, against spiritual wickedness in high places.

                                                    Ephesians 6:12 KJV

What is that written, spray painted on,
Done in the dark, between twilight and dawn.

                                                    Devil's tongues.

Set there before us, to boast, instill fear,
A warning to all, not to come near.

                                                    Devil's tongues.

Driven by Satan, sent on a quest,
Marking the town, choosing the best.

                                                    With devil's tongues.

Taking it back, that's why we pray,
Wickedness in high places,
Step out of the way.
Soap, paint and sanding never will stand,
Only sanctification through the Blood of the Lamb.

A change in gang activity
can only be made
through prayer.

INTIMATE

He that dwelleth in the secret place of the most High shall abide under the shadow of the Almighty.

Psalm 91:1 KJV

Through tender sighs of angel's breath,
I speak to you, my Lord.
You listen intently for my desires,
Protect me from the harsh world around me.
With tongues of praise I call to You,
The faintest sigh you caress.
A love song, flowing tenderly forth, is held,
Oh so gently, in Your mighty arms;
Then returned to me in a River of Peace,
Intimately shared, eternally kept.

WOMAN OF GRACE

Favour is deceitful, and beauty is vain: but a woman that feareth the Lord, she shall be praised.

Born of sacrifice,
    Birthed in grace,
    Bone of man's bone,
    Blood of man's blood.

Chosen to serve,
    Cleaving to the covenant,
    The promise of Adam,
    The promise of Abraham.

Grace to bring forth,
    The children of promise,
    Destined to call,
    Destined to serve.

Grace to pray truth,
    Into the nation,
    Grace to endure,
    Intercession by day,
    Intercession by night.

Unwavering love,
    Unmerited favor,
    To see past the pain,

Of sin's temporal hand,
To the promise of life,
This side of the cross.

Faith in the truth,
    Abounding with love,
    To believe in the birth,
    To believe in the death,
    Of life and of sin,
    Of Spirit, of soul.

Grace to bloom forth,
    As the rose in the desert,
    With fragrance and velvet,
    From the thorns,
    Rigid arms.

Rising to God,
    In manifest witness,
    Of grace and of mercy,
    In truth from above.

BEHIND YOUR VEIL

And thou shalt hang up the vail under the taches, that thou mayest bring in thither within the vail the ark of the testimony: and the vail shall divide unto you between the holy place and the most holy.

Exodus 26:33 KJV

Pull me back,
Behind Your veil,
For I have ventured out,
Into the land of Giants,
Trying to forge the path,
I *think* You want me to walk.
Yet in this land is confusion,
Not born of You.
In this land is strife,
Not called by Your lips.

Scourge the stubbornness from my soul,
Which says this is the way,
This must be the way.

I know this is the wrong way, Lord,
For 'round about mingle tormenting demons,
Cast from the souls of the dying lost.
Light and darkness may not dwell together.

I humbly step back, Lord,
Behind Your veil.
Repenting of the thoughts,
That I could know Your will.

Behind the veil is perfect peace.
Behind the veil is Grace.

I'll rest my mind and bathe my feet,
Until you open the door,
Preparing my journey.
Leaving no possible doubt
Of the path You have set.

But let me rest,
Behind the veil,
Until You are sure,
I will stray no more.

STREET FIGHT

*For God so loved the world, that he gave his only begotten Son,
that whosoever believeth in him should not perish, but have
everlasting life.*

John 3:16 KJV

I'm strong—I have power,
You're weak—you're nothing.
I could hit you—I could stab you,
You're weak—you're nothing.

These streets are mine—I need nothing,
I don't need food—I don't need a room.
I can do anything—I can do everything,
You're weak—you're nothing.

I could kill you—I could take you're money,
I could destroy everything you have.
I am strong—nothing can touch me,
You're weak—you're nothing.

What's wrong with you, man?
Don't you see me, don't you hear me?
You are at my mercy -
You are a bug in the palm of my hand,
You're weak—you're nothing.

Don't you hear me—can't you see what I am.
I am strong—I am tough—nothing can hurt me.

I need nothing—I need no one -
The streets are mine,
You're weak—you're nothing.

You're different, man—you're different.
You don't fear me—but you're not tough.
You sort of glow, man—are you high,
What are you on, man.

You're different, man—you're different.
I'm tough—I'm mean—but—you're different.
What's in you, man—I don't get it.
I'm mean—but you're looking at me like -
Like—we're old friends, or something.
But—I don't have friends -
There are no friends on the street,
NO—you're weak—you're nothing.

I don't need you—I don't need nobody,
The streets are mine—I live through fear,
No one messes with me.
You're different, man—Who are you?

Don't touch me, man,
No one touches me—Nothing touches me.
I'm mean—the streets are mine,
I'm—strong—I'm -
Who are you?
What are you?

Sit down, man—over here,
Where no one can see.
Tell me again why you aren't afraid,

There's no way You could have been like Me,
No way, man—You're weak—you're—different—you're—

I don't want to change,
I don't need food—I don't need nobody,
People are bad news, man -
People are no good,
Out here I'm king, man,
These are my streets—I'm mean . . .

Don't hold me, man—don't touch me—don't. . . .
Why did you do that -
Why do you care about me.
There's nothing in your world for me,
There's no hope—I'm not like you -
You're not like me,
I *can't* be like you.

Who are you, man—look at me cry,
I don't cry—I'm mean—I'm tough—I'm . . .
Who are you?

Ok, man—Ok.
Tell me again,
Tell me again about this Jesus guy.

MY BROTHER, MY FRIEND

Greater love hath no man than this, that a man lay down his life for his friends.

John 15:13 KJV

I have three small finches. All three are of a different variety. They have nothing in common, except a bright white cage and the normal amenities. Bandit has a red mask across his eyes, Speckle is dark brown with a tan chest and brown speckles, Tangerine has a bright orange beak and legs. They were put together over different times and took turns getting used to each other.

On a normal day they disagree and sit as far apart as they can—tolerating the sharing of their space. But, sometimes the abnormal happens. On occasion Speckle will lay on the bottom of the cage and shudder. He's unable to move one leg. He will fly if startled, but must lean against something to stay upright. He does this by gripping and balancing with one leg while pushing against a tray, bar or basket.

This will go on for days and, as unusual as it seems, it is not the truly amazing issue. What is truly amazing is that when he's on the bottom of the cage, shaking and shuddering, one of the others will sit against him, crying out, while the other flies around the cage, screaming and shrieking. At night, when I check on them, all three will be on the branch, one on either side of the ailing bird, propping him in place so that he can sleep in comfort and safety.

They are so protective and caring of the hurting friend that they even take risks that they would not generally take. Several times I have reached into the cage to stroke Speckle, to pray for him, to hold him. The other two would sit right with him until I was close enough to touch him, then they would fly off until I removed my hand. Immediately they would return to their vigil. After a few days Speckle appears normal again and they all go back to "status quo", fussing with each other and keeping their distance.

So often I see people tolerating each other, but not pull in to the troubled and hurting friend. We call each other brother, we call each other friend, but choose to be busy if we think there is the slightest possibility that our emotions may get caught up in another brother's pain.

Shame on us, Lord, if we fail to have the love and compassion of a handful of caged finches. If I call you brother, if I call you friend, then I pray for the compassion to sit with you when you hurt, to cry out for help to carry on, and for the strength to hold you up until you are strong enough to stand alone once again—as often as you need me.

WHICH SIDE

He that is not with me is against me; and he that gathereth not with me scattereth abroad.

Matthew 12:30 KJV

When tempests boil and turn,
This way and that,
Uprooting all you find sacred,
All you find worthy -
On which side of the cross do you rest?

When your thoughts are so strained,
Fact threatens your hope,
Doubt threatens your faith -
On which side of the cross do you rest?

When your family and friends,
Dwell on sorrows and pain,
Straining joy,
Stretching joy,
Quenching joy -
On which side of the cross do you rest?

When you've let promise down,
To the ones that you love,
To yourself,
To your dreams -
On which side of the cross do you rest?

Do you curse and cry out,
　　Blaming God in the dusk,
　　Screaming "why" in self-pity,
　　In pride?

Or do you lay yourself down,
　　At the foot of the cross,
　　And rest in His promise,
　　His love.

A SINGLE MOMENT
OF PRAYER

*Giving thanks always for all things unto God and the Father
in the name of our Lord Jesus Christ;*
                                        Ephesians 5:20 KJV

I look out into a world,
        of drugs, alcohol and murder.
Fear grips my heart,
        there is no avenue of safety.
What to do, Lord?

A silent prayer,
        eyes closed to the dangers at hand.
A cool breeze flows,
        born in the rising of angel's wings.
Sweet music, somewhere distant,
        ripples closer, from the depths of my soul.
Whispering, Sweet Jesus,
        floating above the circumstance.
A strengthening rises,
        as the Spirit renews it supreme peace.

I gaze out again,
        at what the enemy has wrought.
Fear has faded to compassion,
        terror gave way to love.
Only the tears remain,

knowing that so many will never understand,
the indescribable power
of a single moment of prayer.

WHEN

The Lord keeps showing me, over and over,
    images of the little child that rests inside each
    angry man..

The baby who first discovered
    his fingers and toes,
    or laughed with glee upon his first sighting of a
    butterfly.

The little boy who wiggled through his first haircut,
    he was so proud.

The little boy who brought home weed-flowers
    for his mom to put in a vase.

The cut-out crooked hearts
    with "I love you, daddy" scribbled across.

The little boy who wanted to be a policeman,
    a fireman or the President.

The little boy who learned to ride a bike
and could almost keep up with dad.

The little boy who chewed wild grass
and dreamt of flying a rocket to the moon.

The little boy who made a 100% on his spelling test,
but couldn't quite figure out math.

When did he turn into an angry young man,
bitter, distant and lost.

When did friends become more precious than family,
no matter when, no matter where.

When did Christmas cookies turn to alcohol,
Mother Goose to pornography.

When did alcohol turn to drugs;
to live for, to kill for, to die for.

When did skateboards turn to drive-by shootings,
picnics to funerals,
love to hate.

When did he become an angry young man,
falling deeper and deeper into sin,
into death,
into Hell.

If you look close enough you can see that little boy
through the dazed eyes of drugs.

If you listen carefully you can hear that little boy,
crying out for help, for peace, for love.

If you hug him long enough you will feel the shield
and barriers
      fall away, long enough for him to know,
      someone cares.

And if you walk with him long enough
      you can guide him along the path
      to find that little boy again.

FORTRESS

I can do all things through Christ which strengtheneth me.
Philippians. 4:13 KJV

People always tell me how strong I am,
    Admiring the composure they see.
Yet, inside, Jesus holds the frail
    Shaking bird, praying for safety.

Don't confuse my lack of tears for strength,
    they are dammed up behind stone walls,
    protecting my vulnerable heart.
Don't confuse my serene stance for strength,
    for it is a mask which covers the myriad
    of emotions that are so fragile.

You may never know the real me,
    I hide the guilt and pain and fears so well.
I will never allow you close enough
    for fear that you might hurt me.
I choose to stay in the safety of loneliness.

I have tried to surrender what I have become,
    but, by my own will, I am not strong enough.
Neither are you capable of penetrating the fortress
    the enemy and I have so carefully built.

Lord, Jesus, descending through the wings of a dove,
    strip away the chains, tear down the walls,
    that I may learn to love again.

PURE GOLD

And I will bring the third part through the fire, and will refine
them as silver is refined, and will try them as gold is tried: they
shall call on my name, and I will hear them: I will say, It [is] my
people: and they shall say, The LORD [is] my God.
                                        Zechariah 13:9 KJV

I can see you little children,
I can see the tenderness within.
I see the pain with which you shield it,
Open up and let Me in.

Let Me strip away the torments,
Let Me free the child inside.
Let Me open what's within you,
I'll show you why, for you, I died.

If you could only see with My eyes,
Could see the crown and jewels
                    you hold.
If you could only love with My heart,
You'd know that you're pure gold.

. . . .Pure Gold. . . .PURE GOLD.

CHILD OF MY DESIRE

Trust in the Lord with all thine heart; and lean not unto thine own understanding.

Proverbs 3:5 KJV

In my most tragic moments,
When all I see,
Is unforgivable failure;
When I feel least,
Among all men -
You are there.

When I've done all the right,
That I know to do,
With my best ability,
And still things fail -
I hear You call.

When man labels my ways,
Calling me wicked,
Even in righteousness,
When I want to lay down,
When I want to quit -
You smile and nod "go on."

In my smallest failures,
And grandest dreams,
I feel the conviction of life,
Pulling me down,

Taunting me to give up -
But you pull me into Your lap,
To rest.

Why Lord,
With this ever failing vessel,
Would you lead me on,
In tender love,
As an untiring parent,
Choreographing hope.

You knew me before time was,
You saw me in my Mother's womb,
You knew my success,
You shared the joy,
You saw my guilt,
Yet held me close,
Even though you knew,
What was to come.

My child,
Frail and humble,
I see the heart inside,
Chained and fenced,
Tender, vulnerable.

Look past the vessel,
Surrounding the soul,
Molded dust,
Easily blown,
Easily moved,
Tempted.

Inside lies My Word,
Ready to birth,

The promises made,
Right next to My Spirit,
My seed planted there.

You were created for Me,
The child of My love,
No mistake, not unwanted,
As some say to believe.

You're the child of My chamber,
Fragrant oils,
Sweet savor,
Rising to Heaven.

I wait for you in the night,
I watch for you in the day,
I'm as close as you will hold Me,
Or as far as you should say.

Child of My desire,
Precious one at My feet,
Rest with Me,
All the days of our life.

CALLING

Pray without ceasing.

Thessalonians. 5:17

I see Your smile in the reds and golds of dawn,
Your pleasure in the stillness of the waking morning,
You're calling me, Lord,

Pray.

I see Your hand calm the stress of the moment,
Your tender assurance as situations explode,
You're calling me, Lord,

Pray.

I see Your will in the difficult changes of life,
Your plan unfolds to make a path for my feet,
You're calling me, Lord,

Pray.

I see Your peace in the quiet of the night,
Your Word rests gently in my arms, in my heart,
You're calling me, Lord,

Pray.

I FORGIVE

The Lord hath appeared of old unto me, saying, Yea, I have loved thee with an everlasting love: therefore with lovingkindness have I drawn thee.

Jeremiah 31:3 KJV

Someone carelessly speaks words of pain,
   Showering down and restoring old wounds.
My mind submits to you, Lord,
   I forgive and reach out in love.

But my heart slips deep into a void,
   Refusing to listen,
   Refusing to obey,
   Reuniting the moment with the pain,
   Over and Over.

I struggle with an inner battle,
   Back and forth,
   Praying that my heart
   Will melt in obedience,
   Releasing the hurt inside.

I fast and pray,
   Lord, show me the way.
My own shortcomings,
   Rise up before me.
My spirit grieves,
   Was *I* forgiven?

How could I,
     Forgiven for such as these,
     Not forgive.

How could I,
     Loved, in spite of my shame,
     Not love.

HUMBLE BIRTH

And Joseph also went up from Galilee, out of the city of Nazareth, into Judaea, unto the city of David, which is called Bethlehem; (because he was of the house and lineage of David:) [5] To be taxed with Mary his espoused wife, being great with child. [6] And so it was, that, while they were there, the days were accomplished that she should be delivered. [7] And she brought forth her firstborn son, and wrapped him in swaddling clothes, and laid him in a manger; because there was no room for them in the inn.

Luke 2:4-7 KJV

It wasn't that they had to travel,
    travel was a way of life -
    travel to the place of sacrifice -
    travel to the special feasts.

It wasn't the taxation,
    that too had become a way of life.

It wasn't the number of people -
    traveling to their father's lands -
    waiting—walking—crowding.

It wasn't being heavy with child -
    ready for the precious birth -
    difficult to ride -
    impossible to walk.

It was that all had come together on this
　　momentous occasion,
　　even with careful preparation -
　　not really prepared -
　　for the events to come.

And in all the disappointment of the evening,
　　the kindness of a stranger -
　　a humble and rugged resting place -
　　became the catalyst of a birth.

As the night grew its darkest,
　　the light pierced the sky -
　　to announce the hope -
　　of generations to come.

Cutting the sky, as the pillar of fire,
　　drawing those with the pureness of heart -
　　the star spoke the joy -
　　of the new life to come.

In His earliest moments of life,
　　He, the same as others -
　　tiny perfect fingers -
　　tiny perfect toes -
　　the miracle of birth every parent admires.

Yet, with the sameness came the new,
　　the anointed glow -
　　with the very first breath -
　　drawing God's servants -
　　from near and far.

A humble start—for the humbling of the heart.
No wealth or grandeur—the capture of pride.
The kindness of a stranger—to instill mercy.

And the family of flesh mixed with the family of
Spirit -
surrounding—comforting,
to build a solid foundation of love.

It didn't happen the way they had wanted -
Mary and Joseph -
but it was the plan of God.

Not one moment of His precious life
was wasted,
every moment etched the path of tomorrow's
grace.

So tiny—so frail,
a King was born -
a King sent to gather the humble -
to exhort the meek -
to teach love to all who would listen -
to live—and—to die -
for every precious child -
that has graced God's earth.

PREDATOR

2. For there is nothing covered, that shall not be revealed; neither hid, that shall not be known. 3. Therefore whatsoever ye have spoken in darkness shall be heard in the light; and that which ye have spoken in the ear in closets shall be proclaimed upon the housetops.

LUKE 12:2-3 KJV

What wicked thoughts we conjure.
Demons whisper in our ears,
Vaporous torrents rise in our soul.
Who to share it with?
Who will hasten to evil devices,
Deep into the den of disgrace and deception.

Did you hear. . . .do you know. . . .did you see?
Evil seeds planted in anxious minds.
Is it true? No one knows.
Repented? No one cares,
How wonderfully luscious to seek to destroy.
Did you hear. . . .do you know. . . .did you see?

Yet evil thoughts can be heard,
Wicked works can be seen.
As quickly as the subject's life is shattered,
The predator is caught and displayed.
Sometimes in the sight of man,
Always in the sight of God.

Who will quench this treacherous trail?
Who will walk in light and truth,
Where never will darkness be?
Who will heal the wounded soul,
Who'll free the sin bound man.

Only He that knows the goodness
Inside every tortured soul.
Only those who have planted their feet,
Firmly in His footsteps.

LITTLE CHILD

The Spirit of the Lord is upon me, because he hath anointed me to preach the gospel to the poor; he hath sent me to heal the brokenhearted, to preach deliverance to the captives, and recovering of sight to the blind, to set at liberty them that are bruised, [19] To preach the acceptable year of the Lord.

Luke 4:18-19 KJV

Huddled mass, skin and bone,
Family gone, not a home.
Alcohol, to soothe the pain,
Curb the heat, repel the rain.

The future looks very bleak,
Live day by day, week by week.
Need to change, don't know how,
Need it bad, need it now.

Little child, deep inside,
I am here, I am light,
Come to me,
You'll be free.
I am Jesus.

Every night, fight and steal,
Need the drugs, need to deal.
Seated deep, anger hides,
Worthlessness, fear inside.

Drugs help forget, take you high,
Just for today, it's gone tonight.
Have to stop, too much strife,
I want to love, I want a life.

Little child, deep inside,
I am here, I am light,
Come to me,
You'll be free.
I am Jesus.

Daytime I sleep, nights work the street,
Sometimes it's okay, sometimes I'm beat.
Don't matter to no one, no one to care,
I can't run away, I wouldn't dare.

I still have a family, ran away from that mess,
Afraid to go back, they hate me, I guess.
I want to be wanted, want someone to care,
I need arms to hold me, someone to be there.

Little child, deep inside,
I am here, I am light,
Come to me,
You'll be free.
I am Jesus

Work all day, sometimes nights,
Work is tough, at home we fight.
Plagued by bills, how can we pay,
Sometimes I want to run away.

A wife and kids, they need to be fed,
Would they do better with me dead.
I can't hardly cope with the pressure today,
There must be something, there must be a way.

Little child, deep inside,
I am here, I am light,
Come to me,
You'll be free.
I am Jesus.

Home all day, kids to tend,
House to clean, clothes to mend.
Screaming and fussing, night and day,
I want out, but there's no way.

Husband's late, if he comes home at all.
Drinking and fighting, never does call.
Don't want today, don't want tomorrow,
There must be some way to end this sorrow.

Little child, deep inside,
I am here, I am light,
Come to me,
You'll be free.
I am Jesus.

When it all seems to hard,
When there seems no way out,
When it all seems so hopeless,
Lives of anger and doubt.

There's one who can help you,
He's faithful and strong.
He's waiting to greet you,
Whatever your wrongs.

He is Jesus.

DRY BONES

Again he said unto me, Prophesy upon these bones, and say unto
them, O ye dry bones, hear the word of the Lord.
Ezekiel 37:4 KJV

Could I have bore the pain you carried.
Would you have tread where I once walked.
Had we been given each other trials,
Would I or you have chosen different paths,
Or could I have carried the burden
For which I have judged you?

The ravens of gossip and deceit,
Help me to strip the smallest,
Most hidden and covered areas of your being.
With a critical tongue and thoughtless sighs,
I chew away your life, bite by bite.
Stripping away the beauty that was you,
Leaving dry parched bones,
Cast into the wasteland.

What have I done?
Can these bones live again?
Can what was stolen ever be returned?

Will you be able to hear Jesus call,
With the cleansing blood of truth,
That can breathe life back into these bones.
Will you let another help that can love
        and nurture your brokenness back to health,

Or have the words of my mouth caused walls of stone,
So tall and deep,
That none may penetrate.

Could I have carried the burdens for which I have
    judged you?
Could I have carried the burden of the pain
    which I have caused you?
If I had only taken the time to see life through your
    walk,

If . . .

PRAISE

For we are unto God a sweet savour of Christ, in them that are
saved, and in them that perish:

2 Corintians 2:15 KJV

Breath of Heaven,
     whispers down,
     soothes,
     caresses,
     covering,
     with sweet oils,
     of the anointing.

The face of God,
     reflects in the tears
     of the worshipper.

Water and oil,
     flowing together,
     drips to the ground.

Called to earth,
     by the sweet fragrance,
     of sacrificed praise;
     sweet,
     fresh,
     Rose of Sharon.

His robe whispers,
    billows,
    whispers,
    as His feet gently tread,
    on Holy Ground.

The Angels sing,
    Holy,
    Holy.

The anointing flows,
    covers,
    soothes,
    caresses.

Holy, Holy,
    as the voice of God,
    reaches the lost,
    and bursts forth,
    once again,
    in Praise.

SWEET PRINCE

And the four beasts had each of them six wings about him; and they were full of eyes within: and they rest not day and night, saying, Holy, holy, holy, Lord God Almighty, which was, and is, and is to come.

Revelation 4:8 KJV

Oh, that I could cup You in my hands and
    give to another to drink.
Oh, that they could taste the sweet water
    that flows through my body and trickles
    gently from my lips.
Gentle Spirit, unbridled, yet housed within
    - what peace you settle here.
Kissed by Heaven
    - Sweet, sweet soul.
My praises could never foster a strong
    enough command to properly honor you.
Dearest friend—treasured Prince
    - could words ever express the love
    You gave to me to share.

THE TRIAL

In my distress I called upon the Lord, and cried unto my God: he heard my voice out of his temple, and my cry came before him, even into his ears.

Psalm 18:6 KJV

I couldn't pray today,
The words wouldn't form in my heart.
The Scripture made no sense,
Blocks of words and numbers.
I didn't know who to call,
It all seemed so confusing.
Crying out—Lord,
What to do,
What to do.
Simple words,
A simple sacred sacrifice.
I praise You, Lord,
I thank You for this trial.
Then, in a moment,
The miracle occurred.
It was Joy,
In the height of the storm,
It was Joy.

THE ROSE

I am the rose of Sharon, and the lily of the valleys.
Song of Solomon2:1 KJV

In the valley of life,
Where Israel and Egypt,
Dwell together,
You walked.

You searched,
This way and that,
For the Pure of Heart,
To call Your own.

In the garden,
Tended by Israel,
Grew a rose.

It grew upward,
Spreading its leaves and petals,
To the light and the warmth,
Of You.

It grew past the thorns,
Through the winds,
During times of drought,
During the flood.

It grew ever up,
Seeking fellowship with You,
Fully opened,
Exposing the tender inner parts,
Deep within.

As You knelt down,
To savor the beautiful blossom,
You blew gently against it,
Sending the sweet fragrance,
Toward the emptiness of Egypt.

Some caught the fragrance,
In their hearts,
And came to share in the joy,
Of the rose,
Joining Israel in victorious praise.

Others were left, only briefly,
As Israel tends the garden of life,
Watering and feeding,
Pruning and grafting,
Preparing once more,
For the opening of a rose.

GENTLE SPIRIT

*But the Lord said unto him, Go thy way: for he is a chosen vessel
unto me, to bear my name before the Gentiles, and kings, and
the children of Israel:*

Acts 9:15 KJV

Oh, Jesus,
work through this vessel.
Spread peace through this church,
settle your children.
Precious Jesus,
precious Jesus.

Close you eyes church,
listen with your spirits,
listen with your souls.
Do you hear it?
Do you feel it?
Gentle Spirit blow.

Feel the cool breeze,
flowing between the saints.
Feel the billow of His robe
caressing you cheek as He passes by.

Reach out to Him,
reach out.
He hesitates a moment,
He turns and touches the tips

of Your outstretched fingers.
Only a moment,
the gentlest touch.

What Heaven.
What joy.
What peace.

Blow, gentle Spirit.
Touch your children.
Precious Jesus,
precious Jesus.

GENTLE

The Holy Spirit,
    what delightful sensations.
Like standing enveloped in a dense morning fog,
    the sound of the world is nearby,
      but the cool, moist blanket keeps you
      at peace and detached.
Like being snuggled inside a warm woolen blanket;
    covered head to toe.
Protected from the sharp bitter cold;
    warmly—softly held.
Like floating in a cool river on a dry, warm day.
The harsh, sharp noises filtered and replaced
    by the sound of rushing water.
And yet, like electricity surging from every point
    in your body, shooting to the center
    and then out through the top.
Sending you boldly, without fear,
    to complete the task at hand.
Oh, Holy Spirit. Gentle us today.

A SOLDIER

For the wisdom of this world is foolishness with God. For it is written, He taketh the wise in their own craftiness. [20] And again, The Lord knoweth the thoughts of the wise, that they are vain.

1 Corinthians 3:19-20 KJV

I have a picture of a young black man in fieldworker's clothes holding a small baby. At the bottom of the picture is a caption "I Cannot Do Great Things, But I Can Do Small Things in a Great Way". The Lord brought me to that picture over and over today. But, how Lord, how can I do small things in a great way? How can I make any size difference in God's Kingdom?

The Bible says that all portions of the Body are essential to the whole body. No one position has greater worth, no one portion has lesser worth. All are called to a position, to serve in a position they have been prepared for. I can do small things in a great way.

I have been called to be a soldier. I'm not a General, I'm not a Captain, I'm not a Lieutenant—I'm a soldier. I will not lead the troops into battle, but I will fight to preserve the Kingdom, I will devote all my abilities to protect the General, the Captain and the Lieutenant. They will never have to worry about looking back for I will be there—and if I fall, my brother/sister will step forward into my place. We will move always forward in battle to make a safe place for those we have yet to meet—those who have not yet heard the truth—those who have yet to come to the Lord.

What can I do as a soldier? How do I battle? How can I do small things in a great way? How?

I am a soldier. I wage war with the words I speak. I can wage war against evil or I can send turmoil among the troops I walk with—all by the words I choose to share. I can speak life or I can speak death. I can spread comfort and healing or I can spread gossip and dissent. I can do small things in a great way? It's my choice.

As a soldier in the Kingdom I have the tremendous responsibility to protect those above me when they are at their most vulnerable. I can scan the horizon while the General prepares the way for those that will follow. I can be the strength to hold his arms, the inspiration for his words, the confidence that allows him to rest.

As a soldier in the Body I can pray a cover of protection over my Pastor and my Church. I can intercede when the spirit of confusion moves into the assembly. I can watch the body while the Pastor is concentrating on delivery of the message—critical to the hearts, prepared and hungry, in the assembly. I can intercede when confusion and fear overcome the musician or soloist. I can set the shield against the attack of the enemy. And, if I feel overwhelmed, I can engage my brothers/sisters to join with me in battle. For it is my job, as a soldier, to pray for a safe haven for the searching to come into. It is my job to pray a cover of protection over those called to provide the atmosphere for the message for those who's hearts have been tendered by Jesus. It is my job to intercede when the enemy attempts to steal away the anointing—so carefully placed. I cannot do great things, but I can do small things in a great way—I can pray.

I can hear the faint whisper of a name and pray. I can see the faint image of a face and immediately begin to intercede. I can be a thousand miles away at the time, or ten thousand miles, it matters not. I can wage a warring battle for a soul in need—even when I have no clue as to the situation at hand. I am not big, but I am mighty. I am not brilliant, but the wisdom of the ages rests within me. I have no material wealth, but I will inherit a jeweled, golden mansion. I am quiet and meek in this world, but determined and confident in spirit. I am not great—I cannot do great things—but I can do small things in a great way. I am a soldier for God.

But—What if I choose to fail? What if I choose to step away and let you carry your burden as well as mine? And what if you choose to leave it to someone else—and so on—and so on—then who will prepare the way for the lost?

SWEET SAVOR

And another angel came and stood at the altar, having a golden censer; and there was given unto him much incense, that he should offer it with the prayers of all saints upon the golden altar which was before the throne. [4] And the smoke of the incense, which came with the prayers of the saints, ascended up before God out of the angel's hand.

Revelation 8:3-4 KJV

The sweet, sweet essence of praise,
drifting to Heaven.
A mist of fruit-filled fragrance,
Sweet Savor—pulling—drifting.

Come and taste of the wind,
taste the Glory.
Voices lifting in victorious harmony,
Sweet Savor—pulling—drifting.

Drink of the love, flowing in the mist,
sacrificed to you, Lord.
Humbly offered in tender words,
Sweet Savor—pulling—drifting.

A resting place for you,
birthed in the hearts of your children.
So simple, yet so sincere,
Sweet Savor—pulling—drifting.

Upward—to You

LORD, REST HERE

For the kingdom of God is not meat and drink; but righteous-
ness, and peace, and joy in the Holy Ghost.

Romans 14:17 KJV

Lord, rest here.
Comfort in this humble home,
Shine with Glory through our prayers,
Lighting the way in our darkest hour.

Lord, rest here.
Sitting beside me as I read Your Word,
Explaining each question
 as I meditate the passage,
Highlighting special scriptures
 when I need an answer.

Lord, rest here.
A misty image as I try to see Your face,
What Heaven must be like;
 green, pure, peaceful,
Content at Your feet.

Lord, rest here.
Set Angels all about for the moments
 when You must leave,
Keep anger and temptation and evil at bay,
Helping us become the people You need.

Lord, rest here.
I could not bear a single day without You,
I could not consider a moment
    without the touch of the spirit,
I could not imagine a thought
    without Your Son in it.

Lord, rest here.
For this child is Yours,
To mold—and shape—and place -
In Your world—in Your Perfect Will.

THE WEDDING SUPPER

And there came unto me one of the seven angels which had the seven vials full of the seven last plagues, and talked with me, saying, Come hither, I will shew thee the bride, the Lamb's wife.
Revelation 21:9 KJV

It is the Wedding Supper of the Lamb,
The places are set,
Awaiting the arrival of the guests.

The tables are spread with linens of pure white,
Carefully embroidered with purples and reds,
Royalty and Sacrifice.

The goblets of gold caress only the finest wine,
The plates are cut crystal,
Reflecting the Glory of God.

Inside her chamber awaits the Bride,
Preparing—Expecting—Envisioning.
She rests with the tender petals of flowers,
Gathered from the fields,
By loving hands,
Sorting—Choosing—Separating,
Only the best for the Lamb.

Fragrant oils saturate the bed chamber,
Spilling into the hallway,
Floating daintily into the room of the feast,

To anoint the guests,
Drawing on intimacy,
With each other,
With God.

Soon the feast will begin,
The guests will arrive,
The vows will be made,
True commitment forever.

And at the moment of peace,
All will be one,
And one will be all.

It is the Marriage Supper of the Bride.

WHAT IF HE . . .

But my God shall supply all your need according to his riches in glory by Christ Jesus.

Philippians 4:19 KJV

What if He hadn't done it that day,
Fashioned our lives with compassion and clay.
What if the Garden had soon been destroyed,
Because of man's sin against God, there deployed.
What if He hadn't called Noah to build,
If He'd thought it easier if all had been killed.
What if He hadn't called Moses to lead,
Had left wayward people to tend Pharaoh's needs.
What if He hadn't sent Manna for food,
But waited 'til man proved righteous and good.
What if He hadn't sent Giants to flight,
If He hadn't called David to stand up and fight.
What if He hadn't sent Joshua to scout,
If all those who went said there was no way out.
What if He hadn't sent people to pray,
Provide for the Prophets, to open the way.
What if He hadn't sent Jesus to die,
Then where, in God's world, would stand you and I.
What if He hadn't resurrected that day,
Come back to earth to show us the way.
And what if He hadn't called you and I,
But left us to sin, to shame and to die.

But He didn't leave us,
Never will the Word reads.
He stands right beside us,
And provides all our needs.

LaVergne, TN USA
09 November 2009
163572LV00001B/24/A